D0904774

The United States

Indiana

Anne Welsbacher
ABDO & Daughters

visit us at
www.abdopub.com

Published by Abdo & Daughters, 4940 Viking Drive, Suite 622, Edina, Minnesota 55435.
Copyright © 1998 by Abdo Consulting Group, Inc., Pentagon Tower, P.O. Box 36036,
Minneapolis, Minnesota 55435 USA. International copyrights reserved in all countries.
No part of this book may be reproduced in any form without written permission from the
publisher.

Printed in the United States.

Cover and Interior Photo credits: Peter Arnold, Inc., SuperStock

Edited by Lori Kinstad Pupeza
Contributing editor Brooke Henderson
Special thanks to our Checkerboard Kids—Aisha Baker, Peter Dumdei, Annie O'Leary

State population statistics taken from the 2000 census, city population statistics taken
from the 1990 census; U.S. Census Bureau. Other sources: *Indiana,* Fradin and Fradin,
Children's Press, Chicago, 1994; America Online, Compton's Living Encyclopedia, 1997;
World Book Encyclopedia, 1990.

Library of Congress Cataloging-in-Publication Data

Welsbacher, Anne, 1955-
    Indiana / Anne Welsbacher.
    p. cm. -- (United States)
    Includes index.
    Summary: Surveys the people, geography, and history of the midwestern
Hoosier State.
    ISBN 1-56239-873-3
    1. Indiana--Juvenile literature. [1. Indiana.] I. Title. II. Series: United
States (Series)
    F526.3.W45   1998
    977.2--dc21
                                       97-20592
                                       CIP
                                     AC

Contents

Welcome to Indiana 4

Fast Facts About Indiana 6

Indiana's Treasures 8

Beginnings 10

Happenings 12

Indiana's People 18

Indiana's Cities 20

Indiana's Land 22

Indiana at Play 24

Indiana at Work 26

Fun Facts 28

Glossary 30

Internet Sites 31

Index 32

Welcome to Indiana

Indiana is called the Hoosier State. When a friend came to visit, Indiana pioneers said, "Who's here?" This might be why it is now called the "Hoosier" state!

Indiana is the smallest state in the midwest. But it has many people. It has many farms, too.

The **Indianapolis 500** is in Indiana. It is a famous car race. People come from all over the country to see it.

Opposite page: The start of the famous Indianapolis 500 car race in 1997.

Fast Facts

INDIANA

Capital and largest city
Indianapolis (731,327 people)
Area
35,936 square miles
(93,074 sq km)
Population
6,080,485 people
Rank: 14th
Statehood
December 11, 1816
(19th state admitted)
Principal rivers
Ohio River
Wabash River
Highest point
In Wayne County;
1,257 feet (383 m)
Motto
Crossroads of America
Song
"On the Banks of the Wabash,
Far Away"
Famous People
Hoagy Carmichael, Theodore
Dreiser, Michael Jackson, Cole
Porter, Ernie Pyle, Booth
Tarkington

*S*tate Flag

*P*eony

*C*ardinal

*T*ulip Tree

About Indiana

The Hoosier State

Lake Michigan

Detail area

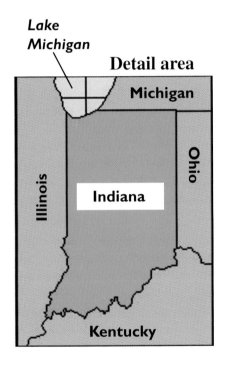

Indiana's abbreviation

Borders: west (Illinois), north (Michigan, Lake Michigan), east (Ohio), south (Kentucky)

Indiana's Treasures

Indiana has **fertile** soil and many lakes and rivers. The best soil is in the northern part of Indiana. It is good for farming. The soil in the south is thinner. It has clay, sand, and silt in it.

Indiana has minerals like coal and limestone. Limestone is used to make cement. Indiana also has gravel.

Summers in Indiana are **humid**. It is cool in the winter and warm in the summer. In the winter it snows in northern Indiana. Sometimes there are **floods** in southern Indiana.

Opposite page: Limestone mining in Indiana.

Beginnings

The first people in Indiana were called **Mound Builders**. They are known for the mounds they built. Some mounds were small. They used them to bury their dead. Other mounds were large. They may have been houses under the ground.

Early Hoosiers were Miami people. In the 1700s, French explorers came. Later, more people came from other states. They were the Delaware, Mahican, Munsee, Shawnee, Kickapoo, Potawatomi, Wea, and Huron.

There was much fighting among the Native Americans and the settlers. Little Turtle, Tecumseh, and the Prophet were three war chiefs who led battles.

The French and the English also fought a war. They fought over Indiana and other land in the Americas. Some Native Americans fought for the French.

In 1816, Indiana became the 19th state. Also in 1816, Abraham Lincoln moved to Indiana. He grew up there. He moved to Illinois in 1830. Later he became President of the United States.

In the 1860s, southern states wanted slavery. Northern states did not. This led to the Civil War. Many Hoosiers fought for the North.

Indiana and other northern states fought slavery another way. They were part of the "**underground railroad**." It wasn't a real railroad. **Abolitionists** helped slaves to escape from their owners. They led them from one house to another. When they got to Canada, they were free.

After the Civil War, many steel mills and other factories were built in Indiana. In 1909, a race track was built. Car racing began in 1911.

Today, Indiana is famous for a car race called the **Indianapolis 500**.

B.C. to 1800s

The First Hoosiers

 1000 B.C.-900 A.D.: Indiana people build hills called **mounds**.

 1680: Miami tribe discovered in Indiana.

 1681: Many Native Americans gather and meet with the French.

 1700s and 1800s: More settlers move to Indiana. More Native Americans come from other states, too.

Indiana

B.C. to 1800s

1790s to 1830s

War Years

1790: Little Turtle leads Miami and other nations in war against white settlers.

1816: Indiana becomes the 19th state.

1830s: Many slaves escaped on the "**underground railroad**" in Indiana and other northern states.

Indiana
1790s to 1830s

1850s to 1970s

Steel and Speed

 1852: The Studebaker brothers open a wagon-making shop in South Bend, Indiana.

 1906: A big steel plant is built in Gary, Indiana.

 1911: The first "**Indy 500**" car race is held.

 1970: The Port of Indiana opens in Burns Harbor. Ships on Lake Michigan can dock in the port.

Indiana
1850s to 1970s

Indiana's People

Indiana has 5.5 million people living there. Many live in **urban** areas. Others live in **rural** areas.

Michael Jackson was born in Gary, Indiana. John Mellencamp was born in Seymour, Indiana. And the famous dancer Twyla Tharp also is from Indiana.

Jim Davis is from Marion, Indiana. He draws the comic strip Garfield.

Wilbur Wright flew the first airplane with his brother Orville. He was born in New Castle, Indiana.

Theodore Dreiser and Booth Tarkington were from Indiana. They were famous writers. The "Hoosier Poet," James Whitcomb Riley, was born in Greenfield, Indiana. The writer Kurt Vonnegut, Jr., is from Indianapolis.

Ryan White was from Indiana. He was a boy who was sick from **AIDS**. Schools would not let him go to classes because he had AIDS. Ryan and his parents fought hard in court and won the right for Ryan to go to school.

The bank robber John Dillinger was from Indiana. David Letterman, the TV show host, is from Indiana. The basketball legend, Larry Bird, is from Indiana, too. He is now the coach of the Indiana Pacers.

Jim Davis

The Wright Brothers

Ryan White

Indiana's Cities

Indianapolis is the largest city in Indiana. It is also the capital of Indiana. It is near the middle of the state.

Fort Wayne is the next largest city. It is in the north part of the state. South Bend is also in the north.

"Gary, Indiana" is the name of a song from the musical, *The Music Man.* Gary is in the far north, near Chicago, Illinois.

Other cities in Indiana are Muncie and Evansville.

The Children's Museum in Indianapolis, Indiana.

Indiana's Land

Indiana is shaped like a sock. The toe sticks out in the southwest part. The heel is at the southeast corner.

Northern Indiana has many lakes and sand dunes. In the center of the state there are farms that grow corn.

To the south are hills and many caves. The Wabash River meets the Ohio River at the southwest corner. The White River runs through the middle of Indiana. It meets up with the Wabash, too.

Lake Michigan is at the northwest corner of Indiana. It is one of the Great Lakes. To the north of Indiana is Michigan. To the east is Ohio. To the south is Kentucky. To the west is Illinois.

Indiana has many kinds of plants and trees. Hickory and oak trees grow there. Trees called cottonwood, Virginia pine, and bald cypress grow in the south. And in sandy areas there are prickly-pear cactuses and orchids!

Some Indiana plants eat bugs! These plants are called the bladderwort, pitcher plant, and round-leaved sundew. Other Indiana plants are pussy willows, violets, peonies, ox-eye daisies, and Queen Anne's lace.

Indiana has many deer, raccoons, and skunks. Quail and wood thrush live in the forests that are all over Indiana. Blue jays, swallows, and cardinals fly throughout the state.

The city of Indianapolis.

Indiana at Play

The Children's Museum in Indianapolis is the largest children's museum in the world. Also in Indianapolis is the Indy Hall of Fame and the race track for the **annual Indianapolis 500** car race. Another annual event in Indianapolis is the state high school basketball championship **tournament**.

Near Lincoln City is the Lincoln Boyhood National Memorial. It has the house where Abraham Lincoln lived as a boy. In Rockport is the Lincoln Pioneer Village.

Indiana has many parks where people can hike and camp. Indiana Dunes National Lakeshore is along Lake Michigan. Wyandotte Cave is one of the largest caves in the United States.

National Lakeshore State Park, Indiana.

Indiana at Work

Many Hoosiers work in service. They sell farm products, food, cars, and other things that people need. They also work in hospitals, hotels, and stores.

A lot of Hoosiers work in **manufacturing**. They make things from steel to other things.

Many people work for the railroad or for truck companies. And others work in public schools.

Some Hoosiers work on farms. Corn is the biggest farm crop. They also grow wheat and hay.

Opposite page: Pouring molten steel in a steel factory in Indiana.

Fun Facts

•Indiana has a town named Santa Claus. It receives many letters for Santa every Christmas.

•The first professional baseball game was played in Fort Wayne, Indiana, in 1871.

•Most of the stone that makes up the Empire State Building came from Indiana! The Empire State Building, in New York City, is one of the tallest buildings in the world.

•Two astronauts came from Indiana. They were Virgil Grissom and Frank Borman.

Opposite page: Raggedy Ann and Andy were born in Indianapolis.

•Raggedy Ann was "born" in Indianapolis in 1914. A girl found her grandmother's old doll. The girl's father added buttons for its eyes. He told stories about the doll. The stories were based on poems by James Whitcomb Riley. Later Raggedy Andy joined his sister.

Glossary

Abolitionist: a person who wanted to abolish or get rid of slavery.

AIDS (Acquired Immunodeficiency Syndrome): a deadly disease with no known cure. The system in the body that keeps a person from getting sick is shut down by the AIDS disease.

Annual: something that happens every year.

Fertile: able to make things grow.

Flood: a lot of rain.

Humid: wet, sticky air.

Indianapolis 500: a famous car race held in Indianapolis.

Manufacture: to make things.

Mound: dirt that covers up something; a mound looks like a small hill.

Mound Builders: ancient people who built mounds.

Rural: in or near the country.

Tournament: a big series of games; the winners of a tournament are the winners for the year.

"Underground railroad": a string of many people's houses; slaves moved from one house to another to get to Canada and freedom.

Urban: in or near a city.

Internet Sites

EcoIndiana
http://www2.inetdirect.net/~ecoindy/intro
Devoted to Indiana's environment and to those organizations active in the restoration, preservation, and defense of our natural heritage.

Indiana Web Directory
http://www.indyguide.com/indyguide
A listing of web sites of Indiana businesses and fun places to visit in Indiana.

Indiana Historical Bureau
http://www.statelib.lib.in.us/www/ihb/ihb.html
Everything you ever wanted to know about the history of Indiana.

These sites are subject to change. Go to your favorite search engine and type in Indiana for more sites.

PASS IT ON

Tell Others Something Special About Your State

To educate readers around the country, pass on interesting tips, places to see, history, and little unknown facts about the state you live in. We want to hear from you!

To get posted on ABDO & Daughters website E-mail us at "mystate@abdopub.com"

Index

A

AIDS 19

C

Canada 11
Civil War 11
coal 8

F

farms 4, 22, 26
forests 23
Fort Wayne 20, 28
French explorers 10

G

Gary 16, 18, 20
Great Lakes 22

H

Hoosier Poet 18

I

Indianapolis 4, 6, 18, 20, 24, 28
Indianapolis 500 4, 11, 24
Indiana's land 22
Indiana's people 18

J

Jackson, Michael 6, 18

L

Lake Michigan 7, 16, 22, 24
lakes 8, 22, 24
limestone 8
Lincoln, Abraham 11, 24

M

manufacturing 26
Miami people 10
midwest 4
minerals 8
Missouri 7
Mound Builders 10

N

Native Americans 10, 12

O

Ohio River 6, 22

P

parks 24
pioneers 4
plants 22, 23

R

rivers 6, 8

S

settlers 10, 12, 14
slavery 11
soil 8
South Bend 16, 20

T

trees 22

U

underground railroad 11, 14

W

Wabash River 6, 22
White, Ryan 19
Wyandotte Cave 24